Please visit our website, www.enslow.com. For a free color catalog of all our high-quality books, call toll free 1-800-398-2504 or fax 1-877-980-4454.

Library of Congress Cataloging-in-Publication Data

Names: Tobler, Elise, 1970– author.
Title: Geckos walk on walls / Elise Tobler.
Description: New York : Enslow Publishing, [2021] | Series: Reptiles rock! | Includes index.
Identifiers: LCCN 2019050714 | ISBN 9781978518186 (library binding) | ISBN 9781978518162 (paperback) | ISBN 9781978518179 (6 Pack) | ISBN 9781978518193 (ebook)
Subjects: LCSH: Geckos—Juvenile literature.
Classification: LCC QL666.L245 T63 2021 | DDC 597.95/2—dc23
LC record available at https://lccn.loc.gov/2019050714

Published in 2021 by
Enslow Publishing
101 West 23rd Street, Suite #240
New York, NY 10011

Copyright © 2021 Enslow Publishing

Designer: Laura Bowen
Editor: Elise Tobler

Photo credits: Cover, p. 1 (gecko) tanoochai/Shutterstock.com; cover, pp. 1–32 (leaves border) Marina Solva/Shutterstock.com; p. 5 Dr. Pixel/Shutterstock.com; p. 6 Sornnarin Nankratok/Shutterstock.com; p. 7 Mr. B-king/Shutterstock.com; p. 8 The World Traveller/Shutterstock.com; p. 9 Cathy Keifer/Shutterstock.com; p. 10 Ian Schofield/Shutterstock.com; p. 11 (top) khlungcenter/Shutterstock.com; p. 11 (bottom) Alessandro Zocc/Shutterstock.com; p. 13 reptiles4all/Shutterstock.com; p. 15 David A. Northcott/Corbis Documentary/Getty Images Plus/Getty Images; p. 16 Matt Jeppson/Shutterstock.com; p. 17 Auscape/UIG/Universal Images Group/Getty Images Plus/Getty Images; p. 19 Sebastian Janicki/Shutterstock.com; p. 21 estivillmi/iStock.com; p. 22 Vitaliy Halenov/iStock.com; p. 23 bbb/Moment Open/Getty Images; p. 25 Peter Hermes Furian/Shutterstock.com; p. 27 MattiaATH/Shutterstock.com; p. 29 Pete Orelup/Moment/Getty Images.

Portions of this work were originally authored by Kathleen Connors and published as *Geckos*. All new material this edition authored by Elise Tobler.

All rights reserved. No part of this book may be reproduced in any form without permission in writing from the publisher, except by a reviewer.

Printed in the United States of America

Some of the images in this book illustrate individuals who are models. The depictions do not imply actual situations or events.

CPSIA compliance information: Batch #BS20ENS: For further information contact Enslow Publishing, New York, New York, at 1-800-398-2504.

CONTENTS

Geckos Are Great! 4
Stick with It. 6
Good Eats 8
The Eyes Have It 10
Can You Hear Me Now? 12
Super Senses. 14
By the Tail. 16
Shedding Skin. 18
Family Matters. 20
Baby Geckos 22
In the Wild. 24
Geckos as Pets 26
Future Geckos. 28
Glossary. 30
For More Information 31
Index. 32

Words in the glossary appear in **bold** type the first time they are used in the text.

GECKOS ARE GREAT

A gecko is a type of lizard that is found in every part of the world except Antarctica. It's too cold for geckos to live there! Geckos can live in rain forests, in deserts, and even on mountains. There are more than 1,850 species, or kinds, of geckos worldwide.

Like many lizards, geckos are ectothermic (ek-toh-THER-mik). That means their body temperature depends on their **environment**. This is why you will often see lizards sunning themselves. It's how they stay warm and keep their blood moving.

Geckos can be smaller than an inch (2.5 cm) or as long as 17 inches (43 cm)!

LEOPARD GECKO

eyelid • nostril • eye • mouth • ear • forelimb • hindlimb • tail

GET THE FACTS!

The world's smallest gecko isn't even an inch (2.5 cm) long! The dwarf gecko is found in the Dominican Republic and on Beata Island, off the southern coast of Hispaniola. The New Caledonian giant gecko is the largest gecko in the world, at 14 to 17 inches (36 to 43 cm).

STICK WITH IT

Geckos have many specialized features, but maybe the most interesting one is the way they can "stick" to many kinds of surfaces. In many places, geckos get inside houses, and it can be hard to chase them out when they can run on walls and ceilings!

Millions of little hairs called setae (SEE-tee) grow on geckos' feet. Each of these hairs splits into even more tiny hairs. The **friction** between these hairs and the wall or leaf the gecko is on is what allows a gecko to stick.

Gecko feet are highly specialized, allowing geckos to cling to surfaces!

GET THE FACTS!

Geckos aren't actually sticky like glue or honey. They can turn their sticking ability on and off, depending on how they move their feet and body.

GOOD EATS

Like many other lizards, geckos love bugs! But unlike other lizards, some kinds of geckos will also eat flowers and fruit. Most pet geckos will eat only bugs, but be sure to check what kind of food they like best.

Geckos tend to prefer live food, not packaged kibble like you would feed a dog or cat. Crickets, flies, and worms are all good options. Geckos usually like to eat at night. Young geckos eat every day, but older geckos often eat only every other day.

In the wild, geckos love to chase and eat bugs.

GET THE FACTS!

Baby geckos can eat up to 20 crickets at one time! Normally, adult geckos will eat 2 to 10 bugs every other day.

THE EYES HAVE IT

Many geckos don't have eyelids you can see. They have a clear **membrane** called a brille that covers the entire surface of their eye. Most geckos don't blink, so if you've ever seen a gecko licking their eye, they are getting the brille wet and cleaning the eye.

Most geckos are nocturnal, which means they are awake and active at night. Their eyes have adapted to work really well in the dark. Gecko eyes are 350 times more **sensitive** to light than human eyes. This allows them to see where they're going and to hunt!

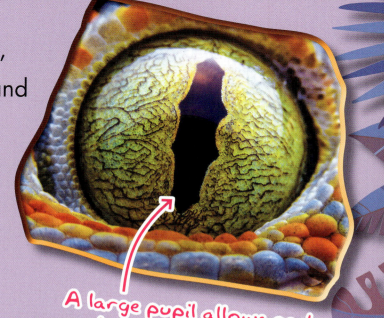

A large pupil allows geckos to see well at night.

GET THE FACTS!

Different parts of the gecko eye work differently, allowing geckos to also see fine in the daylight. Their pupils grow smaller in daylight, looking more like slits, while at night their pupils are wide open.

CAN YOU HEAR ME NOW?

Geckos are the only **reptiles** that "talk." They have the ability to make more than just simple sounds. By clicking their tongue against the roof of their mouth, geckos can make many different kinds of sounds. Geckos may hiss or croak at a predator.

Geckos talk to each other too. They can bark to find a **mate** or to establish territory. Geckos can also locate prey through sound, finding crickets through their songs. Geckos will wait at cricket dens, catching female crickets that have been drawn in by singing males.

Unlike other lizards, geckos can chirp and bark.

GET THE FACTS!

Geckos don't have ears like humans do, so you might not see them right away. They have a small slit usually behind their eye. If you shine a light through one ear, the light will come out through the other ear!

Super Senses

Geckos don't just use their nose to smell the world around them. They also use their tongue! Like snakes, geckos can "taste" the air. They flick their tongue out and then bring it back into their mouth, pressing it against the roof of their mouth, where they have a tasting organ.

Geckos can find food this way and also possible mates. They may also find predators. Geckos also use their tongue to groom themselves, often licking their eye because they don't have an eyelid to do the cleaning work.

Gecko tongues are used for more than just eating!

GET THE FACTS!

The tasting organ in a gecko's mouth is called a Jacobson's organ. This is part of the **olfactory** system. Amphibians, reptiles, and some mammals have this organ, which enables them to taste the air and learn more about their surroundings.

BY THE TAIL

Some species of geckos can "drop" their tail when they are threatened, or feel they are in danger. If a predator catches a gecko by its tail, the gecko can lose its tail and escape. This can also happen if you are holding a pet gecko by the tail—something you should probably try not to do!

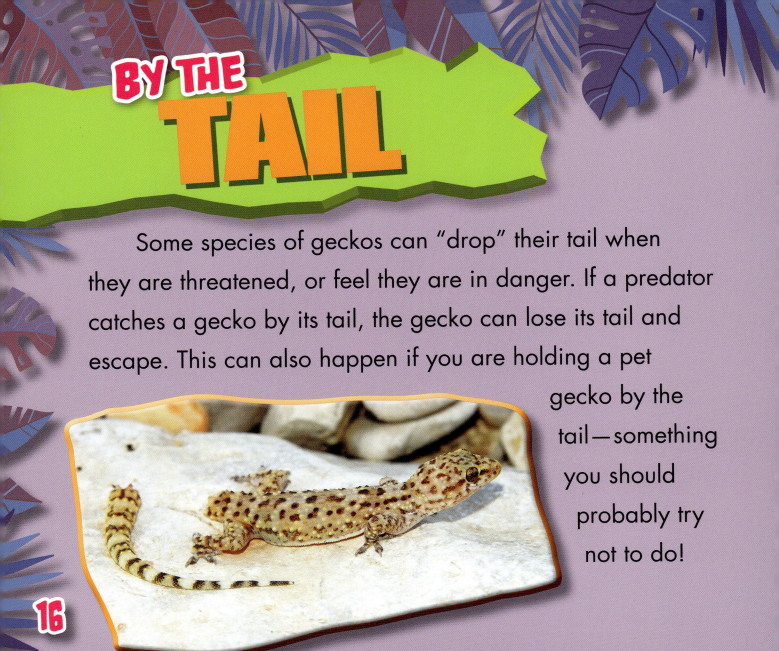

Gecko tails will grow back, but the new tail is often shorter and may not be the same color as the rest of the gecko. Losing a tail can be stressful, and growing it back takes time.

Gecko tails are pretty special in the animal world!

GET THE FACTS!

Tail dropping is considered a defense mechanism. This means that it's an ability geckos have developed to ensure their safety. It allows them to escape alive from dangerous situations, such as attacks from predators or closing doors in a house.

SHEDDING SKIN

You may have seen a snake skin somewhere in the wild. Most reptiles—geckos included—will eventually shed their skin. This process is entirely natural and needed. As the gecko grows, it gets too big for its skin and needs to grow a new one.

Leopard geckos shed their skin all at once. It comes off in one piece, kind of like when you take your pants off. Baby geckos shed their skin a lot because they're growing so fast. Sometimes, geckos will eat their shed skin!

It can take a gecko 24 hours to shed its skin.

GET THE FACTS!

If you have a pet gecko, you can help it shed its skin. You can make sure the gecko has access to wet towels because water helps the skin come off. Leopard geckos can shed as much as once a month!

FAMILY MATTERS

Geckos like to live alone and usually look for other geckos only when it's time to mate. Male geckos will sing songs to tell female geckos it's OK to come closer. Other times of the year, geckos don't invite anyone over, preferring to guard their food.

Female geckos usually lay eggs beneath leaves or dirt, but the tokay gecko will stick its eggs to the sides of trees or rocks. If you see eggs in the wild, it's important not to bother them. Babies will be on the way soon!

GET THE FACTS!

Over 4 to 5 months, female geckos can lay a clutch, or group, of eggs every 15 to 22 days. Burying the eggs helps keep them safe from predators, which include birds, snakes, and frogs.

This mother gecko is guarding her eggs from predators!

BABY GECKOS

Gecko mothers leave before the babies hatch, or come out of their eggs. Baby geckos rely on **instinct** when it comes to knowing what to do. Baby geckos usually shed their first skin when they are born and will eat it. This means they don't have to hunt for food right away.

Eggs kept warm tend to produce male geckos, while cold eggs tend to produce females.

When geckos are ready to hatch, the egg shell will wrinkle. Geckos have an egg tooth to help them cut the shell open. Baby geckos often communicate by wagging their tail when they see other geckos, like puppies do! They can also hiss if they are stressed out.

GET THE FACTS!

Baby geckos eat the same thing adult geckos eat: bugs! But babies need smaller bugs because their mouth and stomach are smaller. Tiny crickets and gnats are perfect. Some pet geckos will eat baby food as a treat!

IN THE WILD

Geckos can live in almost any environment. Leopard geckos are found in deserts. Mediterranean geckos started in Southern Europe and Northern Africa, but now there are big populations in the southern United States. Wild geckos in the United States are usually there because humans let their pet geckos loose.

One amazing kind of gecko is the "flying" gecko. They don't fly like birds! These geckos have flaps of skin that, when they leap from trees, fill with air and allow them to glide and control their fall. Sometimes, they are called "parachute geckos."

WHERE IN THE WORLD?

● gecko range

NORTH AMERICA
EUROPE
ASIA
AFRICA
SOUTH AMERICA
AUSTRALIA
ANTARCTICA

GET THE FACTS!

Geckos are colored to blend into their surroundings, and their skin and scales have adapted to help protect them from predators. Geckos can be yellow, green, brown, blue, orange, and even red!

Geckos live throughout the entire world except in Antarctica.

GECKOS AS PETS

Geckos are wild animals, but they are also kept as pets. If you are considering a gecko as a pet, you will want one that was born in **captivity** and not taken from the wild. Wild animals can have diseases.

You can check with your local pet store about the perfect gecko habitat, or place for it to live. Geckos like to be warm, and remember, they like to be alone. Never keep two male geckos in the same tank, as they may fight with each other. Geckos, like other animals, need special care.

Geckos aren't cuddly like cats, but they can make great pets.

GET THE FACTS!

As pets, geckos can live for 10 to 20 years, so if you get a gecko now, you may still have it when you're ready for college! As with any pet, a gecko is a big responsibility.

FUTURE GECKOS

Geckos become **endangered** when their environment is harmed or changed. Geckos are also being hunted for the value they may bring to doctors and medicine. People are hunting them to sell them. Sometimes, countries set limits as to how many geckos can be hunted.

In the Caribbean, the Union Island gecko has been given special protections because this island is the only place it lives. This will stop the gecko from being caught and illegally traded, and hopefully keep it from disappearing in the wild.

Rare and beautiful geckos are often illegally sold and traded.

GET THE FACTS!

As the **climate** of the world changes, the forests, deserts, and mountains where geckos live will also change. The temperature may rise, changing how geckos hunt, eat, and mate. If we protect their habitats, we can protect the geckos.

GLOSSARY

captivity The state of being caged.

climate The usual weather conditions in a particular place or region.

endangered In danger of dying out.

environment The natural world in which an animal lives.

friction Rubbing one thing against another.

instinct An inborn reaction or behavior that aids in survival.

mate One of two animals that come together to make babies.

membrane A thin sheet or layer.

olfactory Of, relating to, or connected with the sense of smell.

reptile An animal covered with scales or plates that breathes air, has a backbone, and lays eggs, such as a turtle, snake, or lizard.

sensitive Easily affected.

FOR MORE INFORMATION

Books

De Vosjoli, Philippe. *The Leopard Gecko Manual: Expert Advice for Keeping and Caring for a Healthy Leopard Gecko.* East Petersburg, PA: CompanionHouse Books, 2017.

Huber, Raymond. *Gecko.* Somerville, MA: Candlewick Press, 2019.

Pulsifer, Tristan. *I Want a Leopard Gecko.* Greenwich, Nova Scotia, Canada: Crimson Hill Books, 2016.

Websites

Easy Science for Kids
easyscienceforkids.com/all-about-geckos/
This site offers facts and photos about geckos.

National Geographic Kids
kids.nationalgeographic.com/animals/reptiles/gecko/
Here, you can learn all about geckos from *National Geographic!*

San Diego Zoo
kids.sandiegozoo.org/animals/gecko
The San Diego Zoo takes you on a tour of their geckos!

Publisher's note to educators and parents: Our editors have carefully reviewed these websites to ensure that they are suitable for students. Many websites change frequently, however, and we cannot guarantee that a site's future contents will continue to meet our high standards of quality and educational value. Be advised that students should be closely supervised whenever they access the internet.

INDEX

baby geckos, 8, 9, 18, 20, 22, 23
color, 17, 25
ears, 13
eggs, 20, 21, 22, 23
eyes, 10, 11, 13, 14
feet, 6, 7
"flying" geckos, 24
food/eating, 8, 9, 18, 22, 23, 29
home/where they live, 4, 24, 29
leopard geckos, 18, 19, 24
Mediterranean geckos, 24

pet geckos, 8, 16, 19, 23, 24, 26, 27
predators, 12, 14, 16, 17, 21, 25
protecting geckos, 28, 29
shedding skin, 18, 19, 22
size, 5
sounds, 12, 23
tails, 16, 17, 23
tasting organ, 14, 15
tokay geckos, 20
tongues, 12, 14
Union Island geckos, 28